Elliot McCruden

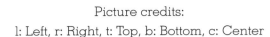

Picture credits:
l: Left, r: Right, t: Top, b: Bottom, c: Center

12t,19: Dan Boman, 16t: Wendy Nero, 16b,17: P&H Mining Equipment Inc.,
18b: Jason Smith, 21t: Gunnar Horpestad, 21b: Fassi Group, 24t: John van de Lustgraaf, Brisbane. Australia,
24b, 25t, 25b, 31t: DaimlerChrysler, 27t, 28b, 32t: Ingemar Eriksson, 30b: Concrete Washout Systems, Inc,
31b: Lakeside Equipment Corporation, 35t: Ruth Harris (http://mysite.wanadoo-members...), 35b: Milepost 92 ½/CORBIS,
36b: AFM-Forest Ltd company, Finland, 37t: Rory Hill, 37b: Per-Erik Nordström, 38t: Martin Greeson,
39t: Spc. Jose Ferrufino, U.S Army, 38-39: DOD, DVIC, 40: Gehl Company/CORBIS, 41: Robert J. Beyers II,
42: Robert Nystrom, 43: http://www.pbase.com/thomaxx/jcb

Copyright: Really Useful Map Company (HK) Ltd.
Published By: Robert Frederick Ltd.
4 North Parade Bath, England.

First Published: 2006

Designed and packaged by
Q2A MEDIA
Printed in China.

CONSTRUCTION VEHICLES

CONTENTS

EARLY DAYS

Huge vehicles like bulldozers and diggers make it easy to construct skyscrapers and other huge buildings. However, until the 20th century people used simple versions of these vehicles to construct buildings, dams and roads.

The Egyptian obelisks were erected using ropes and horses. Hundreds of workers were also employed for the task

Engineering feats

Building awe-inspiring monuments like the Great Wall of China and Stonehenge was a very hard task in ancient times without trucks to carry building material or diggers to make foundations. They did it without cranes to lift heavy stones to the tops of buildings. Instead, workers used spades and ploughs to dig foundations. They used ropes and wood to lift heavy objects and transported building material using boats and ox-drawn carts – all of which required a large amount of manual labour. Construction was a back-breaking task.

Egyptian ramps

Imagine building the Great Pyramid of Giza without construction vehicles. Today this seems impossible, but the ancient Egyptians mined stones, transported them to the site and lifted them – all without trucks or cranes. Workers toiled tirelessly at stone quarries, cutting blocks of stone with chisels, pickaxes and hammers. The stones and other building material were transported to the pyramid construction site either on barges or on ox-drawn wooden sledges.

In ancient Rome, construction workers, usually soldiers, used ploughs, hatchets, sickles, spades and pickaxes to build roads, dams and even the famous Roman aqueducts

Egyptians built inclined stone ramps of polished stone between the Nile and the construction site. They then dragged the stones over the ramp. At the site the stones were drawn up to the desired height on short pieces of wood

The clever Romans

Like the Egyptians, the ancient Romans were great engineers. Without the assistance of construction vehicles, they constructed aqueducts, roads and monuments like the Colosseum at Rome. How the ancient Romans dug tunnels through hills and canals on the ground is still a mystery, but they definitely had no diggers to accomplish such heavy tasks. Nor did they have rollers to level their roads. Instead they used rubble and flat stones to pave roads.

HYDRAULICS AT WORK

Have you wondered how huge vehicles like diggers and cranes are able to work so swiftly and efficiently? These huge machines require a lot of power to perform heavy-duty tasks. The principle behind the working of these vehicles is known as hydraulics.

How it works

Imagine two cylinders containing oil, connected by a narrow pipe, as shown in the picture. When the first cylinder is pushed down, the level of oil in the second cylinder rises because the force applied on the first cylinder is multiplied and transmitted to the second cylinder through the pipe. This is the basic principle used in all hydraulic machinery.

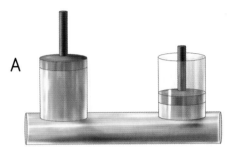

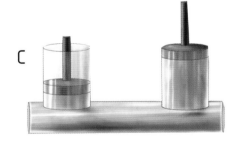

The simple diagram (right) depicts the principle of hydraulics

Basic parts

Any hydraulic machinery will consist of several essential parts. One is a hydraulic pump that pushes the oil into the system. The pump is connected to an engine through gears or belts. Any hydraulic machinery also has an actuator, which is the point where all the action takes place. In the case of a digger, it is the hydraulic cylinder. A control valve helps to direct the fluid into the desired actuator. The oil that is pushed into the cylinder flows back into the pump or, in some cases, a reservoir, where it is filtered for re-use.

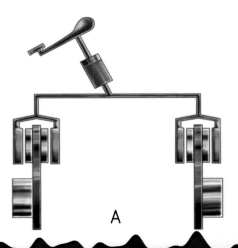

The actuator is the place where all the action takes place in hydraulic machinery

Driven by hydraulics

If you look closely at a digger, you will see that its arm has a pair of long cylinders. These cylinders are attached to a pump containing oil. An engine helps the pump to push oil into the cylinders to work the pistons inside, which in turn move the arm. The control valve determines the amount of oil pumped into the cylinders, thereby controlling the back and forth movement of the arm. The control valve is operated using a joystick inside the cab of the digger.

Hydraulic arm

Driver's cab

Hydraulic cylinders

Construction vehicles like the excavator, or digger, are huge. However, hydraulics help these vehicles to scoop up large amounts of earth and move it around with ease

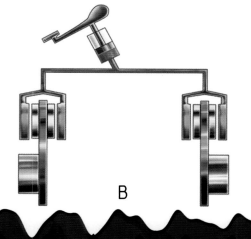

B

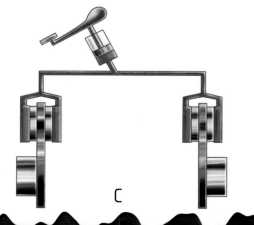

C

BULLDOZERS

The bulldozer is one of the most common construction vehicles. It is a huge tractor fitted with a dozer blade - a large, curved metal plate. Bulldozers are used to remove huge obstacles and remains of structures.

Early bulldozers

The blades of early bulldozers were not curved as they are now

Early bulldozers were simply modified farm tractors. They had a huge metal plate to move layers of soil and their success prompted companies to make proper bulldozers. They were named bulldozers because they were noisy and powerful.

Tracked for success

Imagine driving a large tractor over piles of debris, and moving huge boulders and tons of metal out of the way! Bulldozers are equipped with special parts. Instead of wheels, they have huge metal belts called tracks. The tracks help to distribute the vehicle weight over a larger area, enabling it to move on all types of surface.

The tracks enable the bulldozer to move on sandy and muddy surfaces

Modern bulldozers have rippers that can break the hardest boulders into pieces

Blade

Ripper

Tracks

Mean machine

Modern bulldozers use different types of blades depending upon the work that is to be done. The straight blade (or s-blade) is short and thick, and is used for fine grading. The universal blade (u-blade) is tall and curved. It has large side wings to carry more materials. A combination blade is slightly curved and has smaller side wings. Some bulldozers have huge claw-like equipment at the back, known as a ripper.

SUPER DOZER

The Komatsu D575 is the largest bulldozer in the world. Built by a Japanese company named Komatsu, this bulldozer is used in coal mining. The monstrous vehicle is 4.88 m (16 feet) tall and 11.72 m (38.5 feet) long! Its blade is almost 7.5 m (25 feet) wide.

LOADERS

Loaders are wheeled tractors that have a huge, rectangular bucket in the front to lift and move material. The bucket can be replaced with a mechanical claw-like device to carry loads.

A loader by any name

There are several different types of loaders, such as front, backhoe and skid loaders. Front loaders are usually large with a front bucket mainly used for loading sand and dirt on to trucks and clearing rubble. Sometimes, front loaders are also used for digging. However, they do not make good diggers, as they cannot dig very deep below their wheels.

Loaders can also lift their buckets high up to carry materials short distances

Like in the front loader, the bucket of a skid loader can also be replaced with a snowplough attachment, backhoe or even a concrete pump

Skid loaders

Loaders with fixed tyres that do not turn are called skid loaders. To change direction, the driver changes the spinning speed between the left and right tyres. Skid loaders are smaller and lighter than front loaders but are similar in that they have a wide bucket at the front.

Hydraulic arm

Bucket

Wheels

Backhoe loaders

Backhoe loaders are so called because they have a digging arm at the back, as well as a front bucket. The backhoe can be permanent or removable. Backhoe loaders are more efficient at digging than front loaders and are extensively used for this purpose. They are also used to demolish small structures, transport building materials over short distances and to break asphalt and paved roads. The front bucket sometimes has a detachable bottom that enables the vehicle to empty its load.

▼ Loaders with permanent backhoes have a swivel seat that can turn around to face the backhoe controls

▼ A loader clearing a pathway of snow

PLOUGHING THROUGH SNOW

During winters, loaders are used to remove snow after heavy snowfalls. Skid loaders are especially good for the job, since they are light and can be manoeuvred easily. Special loaders mill the surface of the road with their rough roller attachment, making the road less slippery and safer for vehicles.

DIGGERS

Diggers, or excavators, are used primarily for digging large holes and foundations. They are also used for demolition, heavy-lifting and mining. Diggers have a backhoe and a cab that can rotate on its wheels or tracks.

Types of diggers

There are many varieties of diggers. Some are small and are known as mini or compact diggers. Micro-shovels are diggers that are the size of a motorcycle. They are used to dig and level ground in small, inaccessible places like narrow lanes. Most compact diggers have a small blade attached to the undercarriage that is used for pushing debris away.

Boom

Driver's cab

The backhoe or bucket of a digger can be replaced with other devices like grapplers or breakers

Backhoe

Compact diggers like the one below are used in places where there is little space for movement

Digging deeper

Diggers can be used to dig out mud and silt from sea and riverbeds. This process is called dredging. Dredging is a technique also used when creating new harbours, deepening ports, removing rubbish from sea and river beds and obtaining fresh sand for beaches.

Dredgers

There are many kinds of dredgers. Some dredging jobs require large scale equipment. Large land diggers with specialised crawlers are used to dig sand from riverbeds. The crawler prevents the digger from sinking. Dredging pipes, connected to ships, are often used to suck in silt from the bottom of seas and rivers. Land diggers can also be mounted on pontoons, or barges, for the same purpose. Submersibles with caterpillar tracks, which crawl on the seabed, are used to dig and recover material from the seabed.

MIGHTY DREDGER

The W. D. Fairway is the world's largest dredger. This 173 m-long ship is a suction hopper dredger with a hold called a hopper onboard. The silt that is dredged is dropped into this hopper. Once the hopper is full, the dredger returns to the dumpsite, where the bottom doors of the hopper are opened to empty the silt out.

The term 'dredger' refers not only to land diggers, but also to ships and submersibles that carry out dredging in deeper waters. Dredging ships and submersibles are often used to level the seabed and lay underwater cables

DRAGLINES

Dragline excavators are diggers that are mainly used in strip-mining operations to extract coal and other minerals. Smaller draglines are also used for constructing roads and ports. Draglines are some of the largest vehicles.

Parts of a dragline

A dragline excavator comprises a hoist rope, hoist coupler, dragline bucket, drag coupler and drag rope. Draglines used in mining can move up to 450,000 kg (992,080 pounds) of material at a time! Dragline booms are normally between 45-100 m (148-328 ft) in length. Most draglines do not have wheels or caterpillar tracks. They move by 'walking' with the help of pontoons.

The main difference between draglines and other mining equipment is that the former are not powered by fuel, but electricity. They are usually connected directly to high-voltage grids

Dragline in action

Operating a dragline

Unlike other diggers, draglines do not use hydraulics. The bucket is operated with a hoist and drag ropes. The hoist rope is used to lower and lift the bucket. The bucket is drawn along the surface using the drag rope. The bucket is then swung around to the dumping ground and the drag rope released to tilt the bucket and dump the material.

▸ The mining dragline can drill and deliver well crushed rock to the excavating and loading equipment

Big Muskie

Big Muskie, the largest single-bucket digger in the world was built by Bucyrus-Erie of the United States. This coal-mining dragline was owned by the Central Ohio Coal Company and was as tall as a 22-storey building. It was used in coalmines in Ohio, U.S. for about 22 years and finally dismantled in 1999. The most amazing feature of the dragline - a bucket that could hold more than 10 cars - has been preserved.

LONG WALK!

SUNDEW, one of the biggest draglines in Europe, was built by the British company Ransome and Rapier, and used in quarrying between 1957 and 1974. After it finished work at the first site in Rutland, Northamptonshire, SUNDEW 'walked' to a new site at Corby. The dragline took nine months to cover 21 km (13 miles)!

CRANES

Cranes lift and lower heavy loads. Often seen at construction sites, they are usually stationed temporarily at the site. Cranes can be fixed to the ground or transported to the site whenever they are required.

Cranes from the past

While not as large or varied as modern cranes, cranes of the past played an important role in construction. Cranes were used during the Middle Ages to build castles and cathedrals and to load ships in ports. Some medieval cranes had to be fixed on top of the wall that was being constructed while workers ran large wheels on either side to power the crane.

▶ Medieval cranes, like the one in the picture below, were usually made of wood

▶ Cranes come in various sizes and forms. Their functions also differ greatly, but all cranes consist of a jib and a lifting cable

Jib

Tracks

Counter weight

Crane parts

Every crane stands on a supporting base and rotates using a slewing unit or motor. The jib, an extension of the boom, is the arm of the crane that lifts the load. A trolley runs along the jib to help move the load. Cranes are usually operated from the cab but some have a push-button control station at the base, while others can be operated from a remote station using infrared or radio signals.

Cranes can lift extremely heavy loads including large shipping containers and vehicles

Working a hydraulic crane

The commonly used crane comprises two-gear pumps to pressurise the oil. When pressure increases, the oil flows into cylinders operating the boom of the crane and helps it move up. Releasing pressure brings the boom down. Several cable lines run down the entire length of the boom and jib and are connected to a metal ball that pulls them tight when not carrying loads. A gear under the operator's cab helps to turn the boom around. This is controlled using hydraulic foot-pedals in the cab. Outriggers and counterweights help to balance the crane.

A MONUMENTAL TASK

The Egyptian obelisk at St. Peter's Square in the Vatican was transported to the Square in 1586 by Domenico Fontana, an Italian architect. It took about 40 winches, 75 horses, a huge wooden tower and almost a thousand men to lift the obelisk and stand it upright in the Square.

CRANE MANIA

The most common types of cranes are mobile, telescopic tower, gantry, stacker and floating cranes. Gantry and stacker cranes are not used for construction but, instead, are used in manufacturing and in ports for loading and unloading

Mobile cranes

The most basic cranes are mobile cranes, comprising a boom mounted on a mobile carrier such as a truck or caterpillar tracks. The boom of the crane can be raised and lowered on hinges at the bottom, using cables and pulleys or even hydraulic cylinders, as in the case of hydraulic truck cranes. A hook suspended from the top of the boom is attached to cables that run through the length of the boom. Mobile cranes can be used for demolition by attaching a huge metal ball to the hook, or converted into a digger by adding a bucket

Tower cranes

Tower cranes are used in the construction of tall buildings. Fixed to the ground and taller than the structure that is to be built, tower cranes comprise a vertical tower and a horizontal boom. The long arm of the boom carries the load, while the short arm carries concrete blocks as counterweights. A tower crane is often assembled using a telescopic crane, which comprises a boom divided into many tubes placed one inside another and can be extended or retracted hydraulically.

A crawler crane is mounted on an undercarriage with caterpillar tracks. A rough terrain crane has rubber tyres

Floating cranes

These are used to construct ports and bridges, load and unload ships and even to lift up sunken ships. Floating cranes are mounted on pontoons or barges. Cranes on barges are huge and can lift thousands of tonnes of load, and are preferred for building bridges.

A floating crane building a bridge. Cranes like these are also used to salvage shipwrecks from the bottom of the sea

Telescopic cranes can be attached to transporter vehicles to unload goods upon arrival – in this case onto the roof of a building

STANDING TALL!

The K-10, 000, the largest tower crane in the world, was built by Kroll, a Danish company. At 120 m (394 feet), the crane is nearly three times as tall as the Statue of Liberty. Its boom has a reach of about 90 m (295 feet) and can lift two Challenger tanks. It can withstand wind speeds of over 280km/hour (174 mph).

SCRAPERS

Scrapers are large earth-moving vehicles, similar to diggers and bulldozers, which are mainly used in canal and road construction. However, some scrapers can also be used in agriculture and land levelling.

The beginning

Modern scrapers are based on the revolutionary Fresno scraper, invented by Scottish businessman James Porteous in 1883. Working with farmers in Fresno, California, Porteous realised the need for a faster and more efficient way of building canals in sandy soil and this started him on the design for a new scraper. After discussions with other inventors working on similar designs, Porteous bought their patents to become Fresno Scraper's sole patent holder.

Fresno scrapers were widely used in construction works during the early 1900s. They were even used in the construction of the Panama Canal

James Porteous, the inventor of the Fresno scraper

Revolutionary design

The Fresno scraper scooped up soil instead of pushing it along the ground, like similar machines of its time. Porteous' scraper had a C-shaped bowl with a blade attached along the bottom. The scraper was pulled by horses while the operator walked behind holding its handle. Lifting the handle made the blade cut into soil and load it into the bowl. When the bowl was full, the operator lowered the handle to tilt it up. The operator could change the angle of the bowl using the handle, thereby depositing soil anywhere.

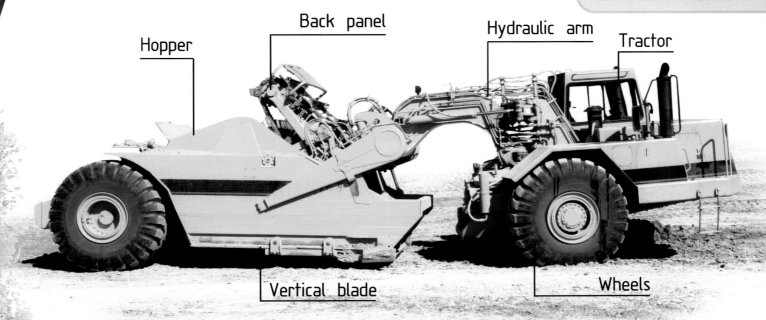

Hopper

Back panel

Hydraulic arm

Tractor

Vertical blade

Wheels

A modern scraper, such as the one in the picture above, is used extensively in the construction of canals and roads

Scraper at work

Modern scrapers consist of a hopper and a tractor that moves it up and down using hydraulics. When the hopper is lowered, the front part cuts into the soil and loads it into the hopper. When full, the operator raises the hopper. A vertical blade prevents the soil from falling out. At the destination, the vertical blade is opened and the hopper's back panel pushed forward to unload the soil. Today, there are many kinds of scrapers including open bowl scrapers, tandem scrapers, elevating and auger scrapers.

TYPES OF SCRAPERS

Open bowl scrapers have a push-cat that helps to load material by pushing the scraper. Tandem scrapers have two engines. The extra power is needed in steep or slippery places. Elevating and auger scrapers are self-loading. They have a looping device that loads the material into the bowl.

TRUCKS

Moving heavy loads over land has been a lot easier since the invention of the wheel. Today, we use trucks of all sizes to transport building materials to and from construction sites. Trucks are even used to transport huge cranes and diggers from one site to another.

Steam trucks like this one were once commonly used to transport goods from one place to another

Early trucks

Trucks came into existence after the invention of the steam engine. Until then, horse-drawn carriages were the fastest mode of transport. By the mid-1800s steam trucks, which were faster and could carry heavy loads, became popular. However, the roads of the time did not allow for long distance transport. Steam trucks were, therefore, used only to carry goods from the factory to the nearest train station or port.

Towards a brighter future

In 1898, Gottlieb Daimler built the first internal combustion engine. This new invention gave trucks more power and increased load capacity. After World War I, many more inventions such as pneumatic tyres, power brakes and six-cylinder engines came into use. This also revolutionised truck design and carrying capacity. Soon, the first modern semi-trailers made their appearance.

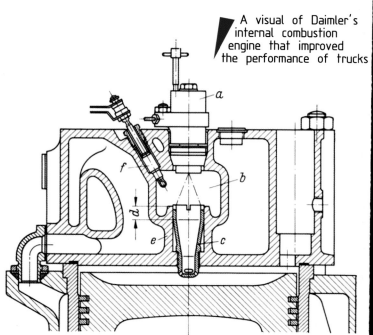

A visual of Daimler's internal combustion engine that improved the performance of trucks

Larger trucks are often used for transporting smaller vehicles to construction sites – sometimes on specially designed trailers, as in the picture above

Parts of a truck

All modern trucks comprise a chassis, a cab, axles, wheels, suspension and an engine. The steel or aluminium chassis forms the framework of the truck to which other parts are attached. The cab is the enclosed space for the driver. Some trucks have a sleeper attached to the cab for the driver to rest in when they're not driving. Most modern trucks use diesel engines. Light trucks such as pickup trucks, however, use petrol engines.

MONSTER TRUCK

The Terex Titan is the largest tandem-axle dump truck in the world. Built by General Motors in 1974, it was used in the coalmine at Sparwood in British Columbia, Canada. The 235 ton monster truck is powered by a 16-cylinder engine. It is 20 m (66 feet) long and has a width of 7.57m (24'10"). Its tyres are about 3.35 m (11 feet) in diameter.

HEAVY-DUTY WORK

Depending upon their size, trucks can be broadly classified into light, medium and heavy categories. Each type has its specific functions. Those used in construction are usually medium or heavy trucks.

Light trucks can carry a surprising amount of cargo, although it is not advisable to overload a vehicle, such as in the picture above

Light trucks

Light trucks are usually considered to be vehicles weighing about 6,000 kg (13,000 pounds) that are used for household and light commercial purposes. Pickup trucks and sports utility vehicles (SUVs) are the most popular light trucks in the world. Pickup trucks are commonly used as an everyday utility vehicle to carry a fair amount of load. They are also used commercially to carry vegetables, fruits and so on. SUVs are designed like station wagons, but are capable of driving on rough terrain. They are also popular as passenger vehicles.

Medium trucks

These trucks weigh between 6,000 kg (13,000 pounds) and 15,000 kg (33,000 pounds). Dump trucks and rubbish trucks are medium trucks. Dump trucks are used for carrying sand and gravel. Some are used in mining and other heavy-duty work. Rubbish trucks are used to carry household garbage and industrial waste to land fills.

Heavy trucks

Trucks larger than medium trucks, that carry heavy loads over long distances, are known as heavy trucks. Heavy trucks are often fitted with trailers. Those that are built for rough terrain driving are called off-road trucks and are mainly used for logging, mining and construction work.

Large off-road trucks are often fitted with trailers to carry logs from the logging site

Large rubbish trucks are used at demolition sites to collect and transfer waste material to recycling plants

MASSIVE MINER

The Liebherr T 282B is the largest operating truck in the world, today. It is used in coal, copper, iron and gold mines across the world. This massive earth-hauling truck is 14.5 m (47.5 feet) long and 7.5 m (25 feet) tall. It can carry loads up to 365 tonnes and travel at a maximum speed of 65 km/hour (40mph). This off-road truck is so huge that it is not allowed on public roads.

DUMP TRUCKS

Dump trucks are used to carry sand, gravel, rocks, bricks and other loads, to and from construction sites.

Dumping loads

A dump truck usually comprises an open box that is operated hydraulically. The outer edge of the box is attached to the back of the truck, but its inner edge can be lifted to "dump" materials at the site. Different dump trucks perform different tasks.

Trailer dump trucks

These trucks consist of a trailer that is pulled by a tractor. A semi-end dump truck has a trailer with a hydraulic hoist that tips the trailer. The bottom dump truck has the dump gate at the bottom of the trailer. The containers have sloping sides so that the material can be off-loaded through the bottom by opening the gate.

Dump box

A standard dump truck has a dump box mounted on the truck's chassis. The hydraulic ram between the cab and the dump box lifts the box when material has to be off-loaded

Hydraulic cylinder

Driver's cab

Other dump trucks

Side dump trucks are trailer dump trucks with hydraulic rams that tip the box to either side while off-loading. Dump trucks with crawlers are used on muddy and uneven sites. These trucks can be easily manoeuvred in narrow spaces by turning their upper parts around.

MONSTER DUMP TRUCKS

Off-road dump trucks are used at coal and diamond mines to carry heavy loads across uneven paths. In some mines, super large dump trucks are required for the extremely heavy payload. These vehicles can be over 45 feet long and 20 feet tall, with tyres twice as high as an adult.

Off-road dump trucks are huge and used mainly at mining sites to haul heavy dirt and rocks

MIXERS

A concrete mixer is one of the most common machines seen at any construction site. It is used to make concrete by mixing cement, sand and water. Some concrete mixers are small enough to be moved manually. Large concrete mixers mounted on trucks are used for heavy construction work.

Portable mixers

A concrete mixer consists of a drum that revolves to mix the various substances used to make concrete. Small portable mixers have wheels that help to move them around. The drum is rotated using electricity. Cement, sand and water are poured in to the drum manually. Once the concrete is mixed thoroughly, the drum is tilted to pour the mixture out.

Mixer trucks

Truck-mounted concrete mixers are one of the most widely used construction vehicles. They consist of a large revolving drum that is filled with ready-to-mix concrete at the factory. As the truck is driven to the construction site, the drum keeps revolving in order to prevent the concrete from hardening.

A truck-mounted concrete mixer dumping concrete at the site

A portable concrete mixer at a construction site

The design of modern screw pumps, used to pump sewage in sewage treatment plants, is based on the principle of the Archimedes' screw

Concrete mixer trucks are now as common as bulldozers and cranes. No building construction is complete without the help of these vehicles

Mixers at work

The dry concrete mix is poured into the drum through a trough attached to the truck. The drum contains a spiral screw, which is used to mix the concrete and then to push it up and out of the drum by rotating the drum in the opposite direction.

THE ARCHIMEDES' SCREW

Concrete mixer trucks work on the principle of the Archimedes' screw, a simple machine devised by the Greek inventor Archimedes, to pump water up from low-lying areas. The machine comprises a screw placed inside a hollow pipe, one end of which is placed in water. The screw is then turned manually. The bottom end of the screw scoops up water which slides up the pipe and falls out of the top, as the screw turns.

SNOWPLOUGH

Some construction vehicles can be fitted with snowploughs to remove snow or ice from roads. However, in places that receive heavy snowfall, specialised snowploughing vehicles are used.

Snowplough trucks are often equipped with Global Positioning Systems and infrared cameras to help the driver find his way even during heavy snowfall

Removing snow

Small trucks or tractors, with a rectangular blade attached in front, are often used to clear snow from pavements and neighbourhood roads. Places with heavy snowfall use dump trucks with a wide, rectangular bucket in front that scoops up the snow and dumps it into the rear box. These trucks also carry salt and other chemicals to melt the snow.

Snow blowers

A snow blower sucks in snow through the auger and blows it to one side through the impeller. They can be single stage or two-stage snow blowers. A single stage blower has only one auger to suck in the snow and discharge it. Two-stage blowers have two or more low-speed augers that suck in the snow and a high-speed impeller to discharge it.

A two-stage snow blower

Impeller

Engine

Auger

Handle

Tracks

Rotary snowploughs

Rotary snowploughs remove snow from railway tracks. The plough consists of a large 'fan' that is propelled by diesel engines or electricity. One or more locomotives push the plough along the tracks while the blades of the fan cut through the snow and suck it in. The snow is then discharged to either side through output chutes at the top of the plough.

A rotary snowplough

A man using a portable snow blower to remove snow

FIGHTING ICE
Accidents on icy roads are one of the biggest dangers during winters. Some dump trucks are used specially for the purpose of making roads less slippery. These trucks carry salt, sand and other chemicals that are discharged through pumps to melt the ice. Loaders attached with rough rollers make roads less slippery by milling the icy surface.

ROAD CONSTRUCTION

Road construction requires specialised vehicles that help to flatten uneven surfaces and pave roads. Some of the most common construction vehicles, such as loaders and diggers, are used during road construction.

Graders

A grader consists of an engine and a cab at the rear, while a blade placed between the front and rear tyres is used to flatten uneven surfaces. They are largely used to prepare a base during road construction. Once the grader has done its work, the road is paved with other materials like asphalt.

Graders are also used to maintain unpaved roads and create flat surfaces before building construction

Roller-compactors

Roller-compactors are popularly known as road-rollers. They are used to harden the ground for roads. After the grader has flattened the surface, the road-roller presses pebbles and stones into the ground. After pouring the asphalt, the road-roller is once again used to harden the road. The road-roller is really a tractor with a huge drum in the front. Smaller road-rollers are used for paving. They have a lever that can be operated by hand.

Most road-rollers have one drum at the front. Some have two drums, one to the front and one to the rear

Making railway lines

Special vehicles are used in the construction and maintenance of railway tracks. A clearance car is used to make sure that trains travelling on a certain track do not face any obstruction. It consists of rods that extend in all directions and move to indicate any obstruction. A liner car is used to maintain the amount of stones and gravel between tracks. A tie-tamper presses gravel into the ground.

STEAMROLLERED!
The steamroller was the precursor to modern road-rollers. It comprised a large tractor with a heavy, iron cylinder that worked as front wheel, much like the modern road-roller. Steamrollers were powered by steam engines.

▼ A tie-tamper being used to press the ties, or sleepers, into the gravel between the tracks

▼ Steamrollers like this one were once used to pave roads. These road-rollers were powered by steam and were slow compared to modern rollers

FORESTRY VEHICLES

Sometimes, large parts of a forest or woods have to be cleared to make way for new buildings, roads, railway lines or bridges. This is done using special vehicles like feller bunchers, harvesters, skidders and forwarders.

A harvester can either be wheeled or tracked, depending on the kind of surface it is used on

Harvesters

Harvesters cut trees and trim their branches. They are widely used throughout the world to fell trees. A harvester head consists of a hydraulic chainsaw that cuts the tree. It is attached to the boom on the vehicle. It also has curved, de-limbing knives used to remove branches from the trunk. A pair of feed-rollers helps to grasp the tree while it is being cut.

Feller bunchers

Some countries use a vehicle called a feller buncher instead of a harvester. This vehicle has a circular saw that spins to cut through the tree. Some feller bunchers have a shear-like device that can be used to cut small trees. A mechanical hand holds the tree at its base while cutting.

Unlike harvesters, feller bunchers do not remove the branches

SKIDDERS OF THE PAST

During the nineteenth century, skidders consisted of a cart pulled by horses or mules. The cart was positioned over the logs that had to be transported. A pair of tongs was used to lift one end of the log. The cart was then pulled forward, causing the log to "skid" along the ground, giving the vehicle its name.

Moving logs

Once the trees are cut, they are transported from the site using forwarders. A forwarder consists of a crane that picks up the logs and places them on a carrier attached to the driver's cab. In places where feller bunchers cut trees, skidders are used for the job. A skidder is a wheeled tractor with a winch to drag logs. It has a small blade in the front to push logs out of the way.

Forwarders are usually used along with harvesters

Some skidders have a hydraulic grapple that lifts one end of the logs to drag them to the collection point, where they are loaded on to trucks

ARMOURED VEHICLES

Combat engineering involves dangerous tasks like laying and detecting landmines, building bridges and clearing the way for combat troops. Vehicles used for such tasks have to be tough and heavily armoured.

Combat engineering vehicles

Vehicles used by the armies of the world for construction and demolition are called combat engineering vehicles, or CEVs. Most CEVs are armoured and based on a tank chassis, and are typically equipped with dozer blades, cranes and winches. Some are used to lay and detect mines, while others carry combat engineer troops to the front. CEVs are usually armed with machine guns and grenade launchers.

Some CEVs are specially built for combat use and can help to dig anti-tank ditches, build roads, remove blocks and create routes through water obstacles

Bridging gaps

Bridge laying vehicles are usually modified tanks, carrying a hydraulic bridge instead of a turret. The bridge is divided into two or more parts that can be joined together when the troops require it. The tank is first anchored into place. The bridge is then hydraulically extended across the site that needs to be crossed over. It is dismantled once the troops and the tank cross over to the other side.

Armoured bulldozers have been used for digging moats, building fortifications, clearing roadblocks and landmines and creating access routes for troop transport

Civilian vehicles

Sometimes, civilian vehicles, such as bulldozers and cranes, are modified for military use by fitting them with armoured plates and other protective gear. Perhaps the best known are the armoured Caterpillar D9 bulldozers widely used by the Israeli Defence Forces.

A bridgelaying tank at work

THE WORLD WAR II FUNNIES

Funnies were modified military tanks used by Britain during World War II. Developed by Sir Percy Hobart - an expert in armoured warfare - especially for the Normandy Beach Landing, they were named Hobart's funnies in his honour. Considered the predecessors of modern combat engineering vehicles, the Funnies included armoured bulldozers, amphibious DD tanks, bridge-layers and mine clearing and flame throwing tanks.

RECYCLING WASTES

Construction and demolition work generates a lot of waste that can be recycled. Manufacturers of construction vehicles also make vehicles that assist in recycling.

Mobile crushers

Mobile crushers are huge machines that can crush leftover concrete, rocks and metal into small pieces fit for reuse. They have a huge container with powerful jaws that can crush the strongest of materials including metallic beams and machinery. A rectangular bucket feeds the debris into this container.

Recycling wood

Wood chippers and grinders assist in recycling 'green' waste. Chippers are small portable machines that can cut tree trunks, branches and brush into small wood chips. Horizontal (or tub) grinders are used for largescale operations. Tree trunks, branches, stumps, roots and brush are fed into the circular 'tub' - the box of the grinder: the machine grinds the material into tiny pieces of wood, which are used as fertiliser.

In tub grinders, the material is put into the tub using a grapple or a large rectangular bucket, while in horizontal grinders a conveyor belt feeds the long grinder. The crushed pieces come out of the machine through a conveyor belt

A road-roller being used to flatten waste in a land fill. This method helps to accommodate a larger amount of waste

Vehicles at landfills

Many vehicles like diggers, rollers, graders and loaders are used at landfills for waste management. Waste materials at construction and demolition sites are sorted into those that can be recycled and those that cannot. The non-recyclables are dumped in huge pits, or landfills, using diggers and loaders, and then flattened with graders and rollers, so that more can be accommodated. Once the landfills are full, they are covered with soil. Construction vehicles are also used at transfer and recycling stations to move and recycle waste.

LANDFILL LESS!
In Europe and other parts of the world, new laws are trying to reduce the amount of landfil allowed because of the environmental damage it causes. Pressure groups - such as Friends of the Earth - call for greater levels of recycling as an alternative, as well as a reduction in waste incineration.

MANUFACTURERS

There are thousands of companies around the world that manufacture construction vehicles. However, some are better known than others for their long presence in the market and for having built some of the biggest construction vehicles in history.

Caterpillar vehicles are easily identified by their caterpillar tracks and their trademark colour

Caterpillar

This American company is one of the largest manufacturers of construction and mining equipment. Caterpillar came into existence in 1925, following the merger of two construction equipment giants of the time – Holt Manufacturing Company and C.L. Best Gas Traction company. Today, the company makes a wide range of construction vehicles including diggers, bulldozers and trucks. One of the most popular Caterpillar vehicles is the CAT D9 bulldozer.

Komatsu

The Japanese giant was a part of the Takeuchi Mining Industry, established to make mining tools for its parent company. Komatsu became an independent company in 1921. During World War II, the company built military tractors for Japan. After the war, Komatsu, who had until then built only tractors, began to make bulldozers and forklifts. Today, the company also makes mining equipment and holds the record for building the world's largest bulldozer.

JCB

Named after its founder, J. C. Bamford, JCB is a leading manufacturer of construction vehicles in the United Kingdom. Established in 1945, the first vehicle that Bamford built was a farm cart. Today, the company is best known for its range of tractors and backhoes. JCB built the first tractors that could travel at reasonable speeds. Prior to this, tractors were very slow. Consequently, the JCB tractors came to be called FasTrac.

OTHER MANUFACTURING GIANTS

Case Construction Equipment, also know as Case CE
Deere & Company
Volvo Construction Equipment
Ingersoll-Rand
Hitachi Construction Machinery
Koering
Liebherr
Terex
Orenstein and Koppel GmbH
Thunderbird

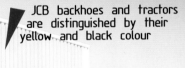

JCB backhoes and tractors are distinguished by their yellow and black colour

Asphalt

A brownish-black solid or semi-solid substance obtained usually as a by-product of petroleum. It is used as a waterproofing agent and to pave roads

Axle

A central shaft between the wheels of a vehicle. It maintains the position of the wheels and also bears the weight of the vehicle and the extra load it carries

Backhoe

A deep, curved shovel-like tool attached to a long mechanical arm used for digging during construction works

Barge

A long, flat-bottomed boat used to carry heavy loads

Boom

The long mechanical arm of a construction vehicle that holds the main tool like a bucket in the case of a digger, or a hook in the case of a crane

Chassis

The basic metallic framework of an automobile consisting of the engine, driveshaft, axles and suspension

Hydraulics

The branch of science that deals with the mechanical properties of liquids. It focuses on the use of fluid properties, such as density, pressure and velocity, in the field of engineering. Hydraulics is used in many day-to-day applications like automobile movement and construction of dams, pipes etc.

Impeller

A rotating device that forces a particular material in a specific direction under pressure

Internal combustion engine

A heat engine in which the fuel burns in a closed space called the combustion chamber. The resulting high temperature and pressure cause the gases in the chamber to expand and in turn act on the pistons or rotors that move the vehicle

Landfill

A waste disposal site, where household rubbish and industrial waste is dumped into large pits and then covered with soil

Outrigger

A heavy projection that is actually an addition to the main structure of a vehicle meant to provide balance to the vehicle or to support another extension

Pneumatic tyres

Tyres that are filled with air. The air in such tyres act as shock absorber when the tyre goes over bumps on roads. These tyres are most commonly used in modern vehicles

Pontoon

A floating device that can be made from metal, concrete or rubber that is used to support aquatic vessels, bridges and certain land vehicles. Pontoons comprise watertight chambers filled with air

Push-cat

A tracked dozer or any similar vehicle that pushes another vehicle like a scraper from behind in order to load the latter with hard material

Quarry

A type of mine from which rock or minerals can be extracted

Snowplough

A device that helps to remove snow. A vehicle equipped with such a device is also called a snowplough

Tracks

Road wheels surrounded by a chain made of alloy steel. Tracks are used instead of wheels in tanks and certain construction vehicles, as they distribute the weight of these vehicles over a larger area thereby preventing the vehicle from sinking into soft ground or snow